John Wesley Powell

by Carolyn Bond

 HOUGHTON MIFFLIN   BOSTON

ILLUSTRATION CREDIT: Susan Carlson

PHOTOGRAPHY CREDITS: Cover © Larry Brownstein/Getty Images Cover; 2–14 (bkgd) © Getty Images; tp © Zach Holmes/Alamy; 2, 4 © Grand Canyon National Park Museum Collection; 5 © Zach Holmes/Alamy; 6 © Douglas Pulsipher/Alamy; 7 © Scott Kemper/Alamy; 9 © Tom O'Connell - Cloudview Images/Alamy; 11 © MONSERRATE J. SCHWARTZ/Alamy; 13 © Jeremy Woodhouse/Getty Images; 14 © Larry Brownstein/Getty Images.

Printed in China

ISBN-13: 978-0-547-02183-6
ISBN-10: 0-547-02183-6

14 15 16 17 0940 19 18 17 16
4500569761

On May 24, 1869, in Green River City, Wyoming, ten brave men climbed into four small boats to begin a daring journey through the Grand Canyon. The leader of the team had only one arm. No one had traveled the entire length of the Grand Canyon before. Many people doubted that the group would live through the trip.

John Wesley Powell was 35 at the time of his journey.

A Natural Leader

John Wesley Powell was the one-armed leader. He had always been adventurous and eager to learn. As a teenager, he had spent a great deal of time reading and exploring.

When the Civil War broke out, he joined the army. During a battle, a bullet ripped through his arm. It had to be removed just below his elbow. Soon afterward, though, he returned to the army for three more years.

In his early twenties, Powell made solo trips down the Illinois, Ohio, and Mississippi rivers.

Powell (on right) and his brother served bravely in the Civil War.

The Journey Begins

Powell had boats specially made for the journey. These boats had special waterproof areas for the group's ==supplies==. In addition to all their food, the boats carried their compasses to help keep them from getting lost as well as instruments to help warn them about the weather.

They named the first canyon they reached Flaming Gorge for the brilliant colors on the rock walls.

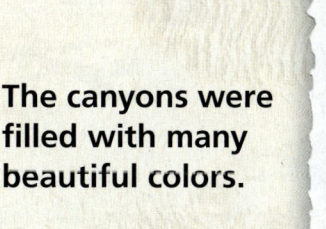

The canyons were filled with many beautiful colors.

After exploring Flaming Gorge for several days, the group moved on. They were about to travel through the first rapids along their <mark>route</mark>. Rapids are places in a river where water is rough and moves quickly. Boats can easily tip over and be smashed on nearby rocks. The men tied the boats together, and they raced through dangerous rapids for several days.

The group spent a few days exploring Flaming Gorge.

Rapids can make a river very dangerous.

The Problems Begin

Sixteen days into the journey, Powell and his crew began to travel into much rougher <mark>territory</mark>. As they tried to row through the dangerous rapids of Lodore Canyon, one of the boats smashed into the rocks. Luckily, no one was killed, but many of the group's supplies were lost.

At several points the men had to empty their boats and carry them along the rocky shore to a safer spot. Then they had to carry the rest of their supplies back to the boats. It was slow, hard work, and the men became discouraged.

Powell encouraged his men to keep going. He reminded them that the government needed to know more about the new territories and was counting on their information.

A Time for Study

Near the end of June, the team finally reached a calmer part of the river, and Powell had the chance to do some exploring. He spent the afternoons making scientific observations and collecting rocks. He also explored several smaller rivers that flowed into the canyon. Along one of these, he discovered the ruins of an ancient city.

Powell and his men explored many interesting areas along the river.

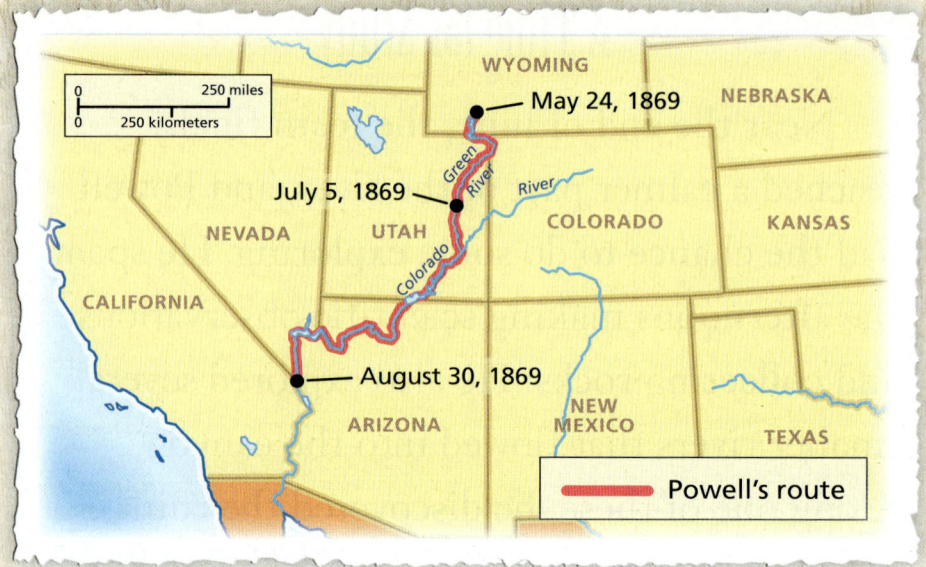

A map of Powell's journey.

The team also met a settlement of Native Americans. Among them, Powell found an interpreter who helped him learn their language. Throughout the rest of his life, Powell took a great interest in Native American peoples and in studying their languages.

As the expedition prepared to leave, Powell got some bad news. Frank Goodman, a member of his crew, had decided to leave the group.

A Real Cliff Hanger

After leaving, the team decided to measure one of the canyon walls. Powell decided to climb up the cliffs. Suddenly, he slipped and was in danger of falling to his death.

Luckily, Powell had asked fellow explorer G. Y. Bradley to **accompany** him. Bradley climbed to a ridge above Powell. Then he used his own pants as a rope to help pull the leader to safety.

Powell was rescued from a canyon cliff like this one.

More Danger and Loss of Crew

For the next month, nearly every day contained a new danger. The rapids became steeper and faster. The canyon walls rose higher and higher above the crew. Storms and floods appeared out of nowhere. Their food began to spoil. Worst of all, the team had no idea how many more days or weeks of danger lay ahead.

On August 27, three more of the men wanted to turn back. Powell tried to change their minds, but the three men refused and left.

Today, the Hoover Dam is at the end of the Grand Canyon.

Success at Last

The rest of Powell's team hurried to complete their journey. Within two days, the expedition reached the end of the Grand Canyon. The expedition was a success. But the three men who had left just days before were not as lucky. They were killed by a group of Native Americans.

Lake Powell is located near the Green River that Powell explored.

After his first trip through the Grand Canyon, Powell made many more expeditions into unknown territory in the West. One of the largest man-made lakes in the world, Lake Powell, is named after him. He also spent the rest of his life learning more about America and its native peoples.

Responding

Main Ideas and Details One of the main ideas about Powell's journey is in the center oval below. What details support this idea? Add details to the chart.

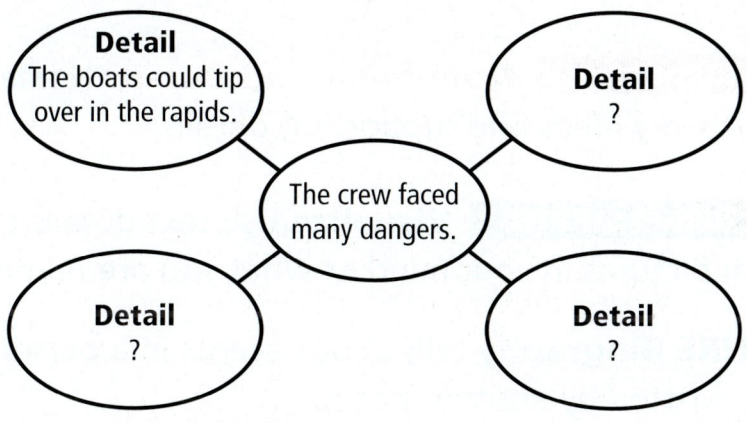

Detail
The boats could tip over in the rapids.

Detail
?

The crew faced many dangers.

Detail
?

Detail
?

Write About It

Text to Self Write a narrative paragraph about a danger you or someone you know has faced. Remember to include interesting, important details.

15

accompany	landmark
clumsy	proposed
corps	route
duty	supplies
interpreter	territory

✔ **TARGET SKILL** **Main Ideas and Details** Name a topic's key ideas and supporting details.

✔ **TARGET STRATEGY** **Visualize** Use text details to form pictures in your mind of what you are reading.

GENRE Biography tells about events in a person's life, written by another person.